THE WINE
GRAFFITI BOOK

First published 1982 by Quiller Press Ltd, 11a Albemarle Street, London W1X 3HE.

ISBN 0 907621 15 5

THE WINE GRAFFITI BOOK

COMPILED BY "THE 4 MUSCATEERS"
FOREWORD BY JOHN ARLOTT
CARTOONS BY JAK, BRISTOW, AND J.P.S.

Designed by J. Partington Smith.
Printed by S. Straker & Sons Ltd.,
Harling House, 47/51 Gt. Suffolk Street, London S.E.1.

FOREWORD

This collection began as a private joke at a dinner the night before the opening of the 1982 Bristol World Wine Fair. It became partly public first through a blackboard beside the W. H. Cullen Wine Club stall at the fair, on which the previous evening's effusions were posted each morning; then through Radio Bristol; and subsequently it received encouragement and a few contributions through **The Times Diary.** Now, offered in print, it has become fully public. Essentially, however, it remains a private joke.

This is not the place to argue the merits of the different wine fairs. It is, though, reasonable to observe that Bristol, the oldest of them is—largely, probably, because it admits the public—the most companionable of them.

Let no reader be depressed at not perceiving the point of some of these offerings at first sight; others of them, perhaps, not at all. Senses of humour are as different as people; and as periods. Perhaps, if you miss some of them, your mind is too pure; or, possibly, not pure enough.

The founder diners emerged into the light of the first morning of the Fair committed, not to the original scheme of a book of graffiti, but to a book of **wine** graffiti. The outcome is a fair indication of the conviviality and humour of those who work in the wine trade. That business has progressed—so they say—since the days when a merchant remarked 'Only the clerks work after lunch in this establishment.' It has become a harder, more competitive—at times cut-throat—field since the actuaries took over control from the wine men. The wine men, though, contrive still to find life amusing; their wines a matter of enthusiasm; the atmosphere—of tasting, dining, imbibing—of the trade, pleasurable; even though the casualty list is murderously high.

The prime movers in this operation were Michael Rayment, whose Lebanese red wine from Château Musar has surprised many people and commands respect within the trade; James Rogers and Paul Tholen of W. H. Cullen, who made a considerable impact on the Fair; Andy Henderson of the rising Spanish power, Torres Wines; and Richard Goodman of the New Zealand entry to the British market, Cook's Wines from Te Kauwhata. They formed the nucleus of the occasionally bibulously reinforced committee which made the final selection from a huge mixed bag of offerings. Others were recruited—JAK to draw the cover cartoon; Frank Dickens (Bristow) and 'J.P.S.' to contribute the caricatures in the text; this harmless and unsuspecting passer-by to write the foreword.

By the end of September the contents had not been fully mustered; yet—such is the faith of those who see production as the rapid passage of bottles through bond—the publication is confidently forecast for 22nd November—and 22nd November **1982**, at that.

A significant proportion of the proceeds will go to the Wine & Spirit Trades Benevolent Society. Its

Committee is working to raise an investment capital of £200,000 by its centenary in 1986. The Society has over two hundred pensioners up and down the country; helps other former employees in need; and has founded a permanent home for many of them. The Vintry estate at Eastbourne, established in 1950, now has 21 semi-detached bungalows for married couples or single persons; and an extension wing for 5 persons no longer able to look after themselves. The compilers hope that the Society's share of the proceeds will be helped by sales in the wineshops, wine bars and, less probably, wine wholesalers.

Graffiti is not new. It existed even before the days of football supporters or aerosols. Indeed, examples found on the walls of Pompeii already indicated some degree of experience. It has never lapsed; but only lately has it surged up to become a—sometimes hilarious—much observed—even studied—facet of the social pattern.

No one has yet offered acceptable analysis or criticism of the literary quality of the Pompeiian inscriptions; most have been happy enough to know that they have survived. Neither is it argued that lengthy effusions in verse constitute graffiti, the (understood) essence of which is brevity (and, desirably, wit). On the other hand, graffiti is (or should it be 'are'?) not expected to scan.

Let it not be thought that our compilers the **'Four Muscateers'** are without conscience. They were not completely unaware that some of their readers might shudder—or feign to shudder—at their humour; as people do, either from revulsion, or simply out of envy at not having thought of it themselves. So, to redeem any possible offence, and with that missionary zeal so often found in hardened drinkers, they have provided a glossary of wine terms; with accompanying guide to pronunciation which may horrify some phoneticists; and even more Frenchmen, Germans, and Italians.

So cherish such worthy aims; if you cannot forgive, do not forget; in this wine establishment only the graffiti writers work after dinner.

John Arlott

October 1982

DRINK RETSINA IF YOU PINE FOR THE PARTHENON

— When in France,
my wife likes to be Chablis
treated! —

'MAGNUM FORCE'
— FRENCH
PARAMILITARY
WING OF THE
APPELLATION
CONTROLEÉ

Musar for Lebanon,
– not Cowes.

BURGLARS ARE
CHIANTI

DOSAGE –
FRANCE'S ANSWER
TO V.D.

No matter what you call it
it ruins many a plan.
It's Brewers droop in Bradford,
and Coq-au-vin in Cannes.

I thought Torres was a load of bull until I discovered Esmeralda.

Spanna goes with nuts!

Mis E.N. Bouteilles loves Dan Snoscaves

MY WIFE'S LIKE A BOTTLE OF WINE— WHEN SHE'S BLUE YOU GET NUN!

V·D·Q·S—
Upmarket
POX!

Chewing Wine Gums gives hangovers to Dentists!

Don't sit down
—Piat d'Or

ASTI SPUMANTE
—ITALIAN
FOR HANGOVER

Don't like water – Sauternes to Wine!

John McEnroe must be a connoisseur 'cos he's always having a 'little wine'!

"FRENCH"
RELAXATION!
– RING
Rosé d'Anjou.

All the wine in this establishment has been passed by the Management!

"WELL-TRODDEN" MUST BE GRAPE FEETIE
GRAPE EXPECTATIONS IS A DICKENS OF A YARN!
EVER TRIED BURGUNDY IN CANS?
– No, but I've been canned in BURGUNDY!
Beer – O.K.
Café – Au Lait
Torres – Olé!

WHAT HAVE RACING DRIVERS GOT AGAINST CHAMPAGNE?
B.R. IN HOC DUE TO DOMESTICA DISPUTE !!
—You must grappa the Rhines, Sauternes out the Reds and Sec the lot of them.
*FOR A ROSÉ FUTURE !?
JPS

Riesling is a Chinese Aphrodisiac!

I'll have a large Port please.
— HOW ABOUT SOUTHAMPTON!

DRINK CHATEAU MUSAR AND CEDAR LEBANON.

HOW DO YOU DOCTOR THE WINE TEMPERATURE? — NURSE THE GLASS!

VILL I VIN? NO SU-SCHLUCK!

Vouvray! Vouvray! Let's have Saumur.

Riesling United 11
Phylloxera 0.

STOP NOBLE ROT
—WEAR A
CONDOM

Gentlemen
prefer
BLANCS !

I ORDERED A BUCKS FIZZ
BUT SHE GAVE ME AN L.P.

Flying west from Lebanon young Kline
drank rather too much Musar wine
He climbed TORRES in Spain
but he fell and was slain
And so COOKS served him
pickled in brine.

Would a wine waiter in 'McDonalds' be a Burger-meister?

SPREAD THE WORD – MARGAUX IS BETTER THAN BUTTER!

I THOUGHT CIRRHOSIS WAS A CLOUD UNTIL I DISCOVERED LIEBFRAUMILCH

A Blanc cheque makes your bank manager see RED!

HOCK THE HERAULT ANGELS SING

AFTER A HEAVY NIGHT IN ANJOU, EVERYTHING IS COMING UP ROSÉ

If man can live to be a hundred, drink DOUBLE CENTURY, and have two bites of the SHERRY!

I THOUGHT 'BRUT' WAS AN AFTERSHAVE UNTIL I DISCOVERED THE BRISTOL WORLD WINE FAIR !

DO BLUE NUNS HAVE PORNOGRAPHIC HABITS ?

VINYARDS
- not
vin METRES!

HOW DO YOU MAKE
AN ALSATAN WINE?
— Pull its tail! —

TOSS A PEBBLE
INTO A WINE LAKE
& YOU GET A LITTLE PLONK!

The wine
in Spain
is TORRESTIAl
in the main!

Old wines
never die,
they just
VINtage!

my old man has a nose for wine — BRIGHT RED.
GRANDMA USED TO THINK SYLVANER WAS A DANCE BAND!
LAST NIGHT I WASHED MY HAIR IN ITALIAN WINE AND NOW I CHIANTI DO A THING WITH IT.
Superman drinks MARTINI Anytime—Anyplace—Anywhere!

FOR A AGGY MEAL COCKS WINES!

PULL A "CORK" & UNWIND!

IS MIXING BLUE NUN WITH WATNEYS, VIRGIN' ON THE REDICULOUS?

Whats wrong with MEdoc?

- you've got a Graves case of a detached Retsina

POURRITURE NOBLE IS THE CONTRIBUTION OF THE UPPER HOUSE

MAD MOSELLE FROM ARMENTIERS — BUVEZ-VOUS?

ROAD WORKS AHEAD — SAUTERNES AT THE NEXT PUB.

MEDOC SAYS CHAMPAGNE IS NOT A GRAVES ILLNESS!

IS IT SOAVE MON SUAVE!

WOULD YOU CALL A GERMAN WINE COMMERCIAL "AD HOC"

I had Rosé in Anjou and, boy was she in the pink!

Vin Rouge – G.P.O. delivery
Vin Blanc – Ambulance
Vin Rose – Interflora
Vin Ordinaire – Ford Transit!

I don't Ventoux appear Saki
but my Chenas
has buried your Beaune!

BE A MUSAR BUSAR

Wine SAUTERNES me on!

MRS THATCHER
LIKES HER CABERNET
WITH A GROUSE.

— YOUR WINE WON'T GO FURTHER BUT YOUR FRIEND MIGHT!

ABSINTHE makes the heart grow fonder.

PORT IS THE WINE OF THE MARITIME LEFT.

Bordeaux

— DISINTERESTED PERRIER WATER.

BORDEAUX
BORE D'EAU ?
BORED DOE ?
BORED ? OH !
BOARD HO
ALL ABOARD HO !
FOR BORDEAUX — UMMMMM !

Cheri on the rocks can be damn uncomfortable !

Pomerol — an Australians idea of an English breakfast !

ANY BLUE NUN ? SORRY YOU'RE OUT OF SCHLUCK !

'MOSAIC' SHERRY PUTS YOU IN THE PICTURE!

Carmen sings — Tomes adores

CORKSCREWS TURN YOU TO WINE

HICK! HOCK! HOORAY!

Planking myself beside her, I tried to take a vintage, but when I painted a rosé future she saw red and I drew a blanc.

OPEN YOUR NEW ZEALAND WINE WITH A 'COOKS' SCREW

THE WINE WAS SO OLD, IT HAD TO BE BROUGHT TO THE TABLE IN A WHEEL CHAIR!

AFTER A TOUR OF THE LOIRE VALLEY....
...I WAS ABSOLUTELY CHATEAUED!

CALIFORNIAN WINE
—the sun shines
out of its glass!!

ORLÉANS   SANCERRE

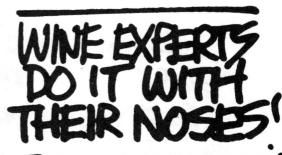

WINE EXPERTS
DO IT WITH
THEIR NOSES!

Was the Grapes of Wrath
a best cellar?

Campers drink
shampers
with intent!

EVERY PITCHER TELLS A STORY

The "Angry Lamb" by MOUTON ROTHSCHILD.

"GAY LUSSAC" IS A FRENCH POOF!

I'D PREFER TO HAVE A FULL BOTTLE
IN FRONT OF ME THAN A
FULL FRONTAL LOBOTOMY!

If you plant sparklet bulbs,
do you get grape Hyacinths'?

Wine's fine.
Liquor's quicker!

Musar
c'est tres
Sheikh

THERE'S PLENTY OF HAIR ON A CAMEL
THERE'S PLENTY OF HAIR ON AN APE
IT'S ONLY THE HAIRS ON A GOOSEBERRY
THAT PREVENT IT FROM BEING A GRAPE!

The sweet wine said
I shan't be a Sec!

CHAMPAGNE GRAFFITI ARE PRETTY KRUG!

Vino Blanco is great for plimsoles!

WINE ON THE TABLE, WINE ON THE BAR,
IF YOU DRINK TOO MUCH YOU WON'T GO FAR!

Is that your CROFT — No, it's mon sherry.

MY WIFE
USED TO WINE
'TIL WE
DISCOVERED
'69'

IF IT'S Tokay by you,
IT'S Tokay by me.

I THOUGHT ORSON WELLES WAS A
SPA TOWN, 'TIL I DISCOVERED SHERRY

Mary had a little lamb?
or was it a Mouton Cadet?

Where's De.Port?
— IN DE-CANTER!

THE TALE OF GEOFFREY CHAMBERTIN
(A mock Herault-ic epic)

Come close and be
  acetic one and all,
and let me tell
  a tale of ancient Gaul,
of Geoffrey Chambertin,
  stout heart and bold,
who rode in search of love
  and wealth untold.

A knight in shining Armagnac
    was he, who looked resplendent
on his trusty steed Cheval Blanc,
    who with Bonnézeaux his dog,
ne'er left his side
    upon his weary slog.

Forsooth our Herault
    seldom wore a smile,
his face was Douro,
    life was quite a trial,
for seven long years he'd
    searched to find his lover
the Maiden Gloria,
    there could be no other.

With heavy heart he saw
    that fateful night,
when Gloria awoke
    in dreadful fright,
to find Phyll Oxera
    the parasite,
had taken her
    while she did vainly fight.

And so our Geoffrey swore
    with utmost zest,
that he would put the
    vile Phyll to death,
so he could lie down
    once again and rest,
against his lover's
    two Gigondas breasts.

That night as he did seek
    a place to stay,
a wonderous smell reached him:
    steak frites Grillet
and there before him
    stood his worthy host
the Müller Thurgau,
    schloss'd as was his wont.

"Chai, what a nice surprise!",
    cried Bouzy Bill,
"Pedro Ximenez,
    fetch our knight some swill,"
and as the servant went
    to fetch some wine,
old Bouzy Bill,
    insisted Geoffrey dine.

The miller turned
    and Geoffrey followed in,
and asked politely
    how the gout had been.
"Damn Gamay leg,
    Medoc's been Fixin it,
it slows me down
    whene'er I chase crumpet."

No sooner said
    than Barbera appeared,
"Anis of mine," the miller said
    and leered,
and as the buxom wench
    set down the tray,
he slapped her Bommes
    and sent her on her way.

"And now good Filhot,
    without more a-doux,
what brings you to these parts,
    give me your news."
With heavy heart
    Sir Geoffrey told his tale
how he had sought his love
    to no avail.

"Why, syrah! she won't take you
    long to find,
Phyll's drunken Irish lackey,
    Jim Haut Brion
is gaoler to the maid
    not far from here,
his master gone for weeks
    to hunt for deer.

SLAP!

"But yet be warned,
    before he did depart,
he made the kindly wizard Merlot
    cast a spell upon
a mighty chasselas belt,
    which strikes down all
who make their presence felt."

"The brut!", Sir Geoffrey cried
    and clenched his fist,
the thought drives me half baumé,
    round the twist.
Please tell me where
    old Merlot can be found,
that we can run
    Phyll Oxera to ground."

"Old Merlot is an Hermitage,"
    said Bill,
he lives all by himself
    upon yon hill,
but come, we're tired,
    we need some sleep old friend,
your bedroom's on the right,
    by the Loudenne."

At dawn he saddled up
  and left alone,
pursued by dog
  still clutching at a Beaune,
and soon he'd found the wizard
  and agreed how best
his Amoroso could be freed.

Then they advanced
  upon the castle keep,
and found the gaoler
  drunk and fast asleep.
The last he knew
  of that historic day
was Geoffrey's Muscat
  blasting him away.

"Sherry, come close," said Geoffrey and he knelt
  forgetting just that once the chasselas belt.
"No, wait!" cried Merlot, "lest you come to harm.
  I must remove
Phyll Oxera's wicked charm."

"Sur lie you know
  the words to set me free?
I can not live
  without my love Geoffrey."
In answer Merlot
  thundered out the spell
"Shiraz! Traminer!
  Riesling! Zinfandel!"

"Retsina!"
  shrieked old Merle in ecstacy,
as Gloria's belt
  broke up about her knees.
"Fair maid, you're free at last.
  Go on, embrace your knight,
and then let's leave
  this dreadful place."

"Corton on the hop, I think!"
  They turned to see
a hand grenache land
  right amidst the three,
and there was Phyll,
  his arms about his sides
convulsed in mirth
  about to see them die.

But Geoffrey acted fast,
  he crossed the flor,
and tossed the hand grenache
  out of the door.
His heckles up, he turned
  and without scruples,
leapt at Phyll
  and grabbed at his Chiroubles.

"Ouch! ouch!" screamed wretched Phyll,
    "please let me go!
"What do you think you're at,
    that's my pinot!"
As Geoffrey,
    with one last gigantic throw,
removed his man for good
    through the window.

That night they all rejoiced
    when Geoffrey said
that Gloria and he
    would shortly wed.
Her parents, Marsala
    and Pape Clement,
were glad to Palmer off
    to this fine gent.

Now as I bring
    this tale to a close,
you're wondering, no doubt,
    how come I know
so much of love,
    as well as vinous things,
the answer's in my name
    —Pomerol Flynn.

SANDEMAN PIESPORT,
BUT DELAFORCE
HAS COCKBURN
AND CAN PINOT MORE!

Cdmans wines
are a ~~MUST~~ !
mustard.

Medoc soon Corton
to my Champagne!

VINTAGE
PORT
ROTS THE
WALLET!

I LIKE
BEDTIME
TORRES!

These Ad hoc Puns are bordeauxing on the Viniculous!

The husbands burden? Entre deux meres

DRINKING TOO MUCH ROSÉ IS D'ANJOU - ROUS

She was only a grape pickers daughter but she was never CHABLIS dressed!

Oporto is the port between two ear holes!

I HEAR THE SOUND OF MOUSSEC

MILK'S GOT A LOT OF BOTTLE
— but wine's got glass distinction!

How about a little sekt?
—Sure, Sauternes down the lane.
—Was that Tokay?
YES, only Meursault
—SAUMUR THEN?

BURGUNDIANS ARE SEX MAD — ALL THEY TALK ABOUT IS PINOTS AND FINISH.

The Grapes of Wrath give me the Pip!

Water has killed more people than wine — remember the flood?

Have you got a white Mâcon? — NO! THESE ARE MY OVERALLS!

Meet me in the vineyards — we'll blend.

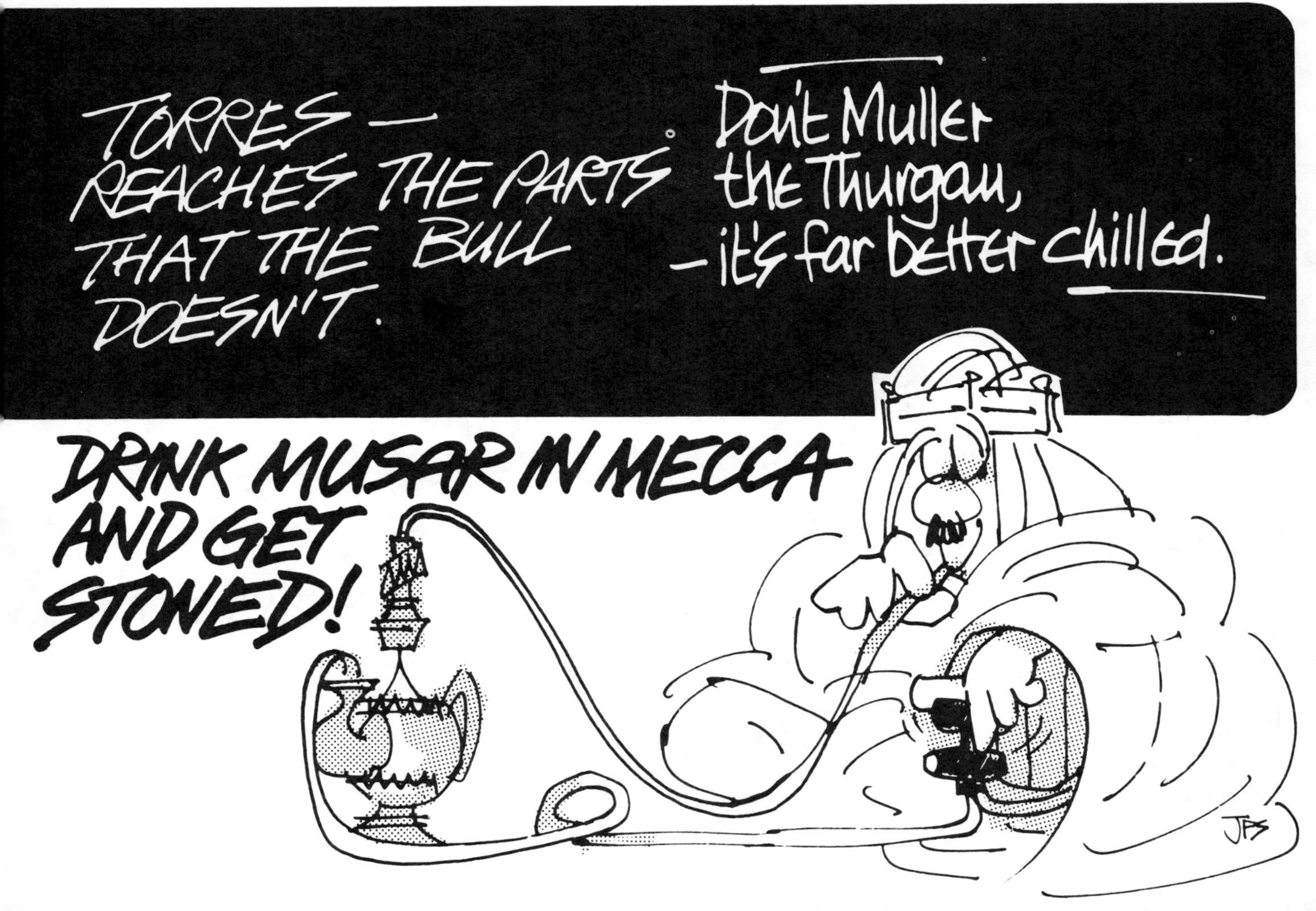
TORRES — REACHES THE PARTS THAT THE BULL DOESN'T.
Don't Muller the Thurgau, — it's far better chilled.
DRINK MUSAR IN MECCA AND GET STONED!
JBS

Dem Beaunes
Dem Beaunes
Dem
Dry Beaunes

Sunday
Pauls
without
Masson.

A Muscadet
keeps the
Doctor away

TE KAUWHATA - Isn't she the Dame that sings Carmen?

The. Irish think Blue Nun
is a porno film.

Grape treaders do not wear old socks.
—I found a marinated toe nail to prove it.

Brenda O'Reilly
the best screw
in Cork

I THOUGHT CHAMBERTIN WAS A POTTY UNTIL I DISCOVERED BURGUNDY

WITH WINE, IT'S THIRST COME, THIRST SERVED!

Pedro Ximinez is really a Mexican Hat Dancer!

Take a Blue Nun to lunch - You'll be amazed!

SECS, SECS, SECS - THAT'S ALL MEN EVER TALK ABOUT!

If Magellan was a straight, what does that make Cook's ?

JACK SPRAT
COULD EAT NO FAT
HIS WIFE
ATE FAT ALONE _
SO WHEN SHE ORDERED
CÔTES de PORCS,
HE ORDERED
CÔTES de BEAUNE.

IT'S A SUBTLE BLEND OF MUSCATELLE AND HOCK — WE CALL IT MUCK!

WHY GROUSE WHEN YOU CAN WINE ?

I Advocaat we keep Mumm, vous Campari ?

SINCE WEARING PERFUME I LIKE TO HAVE MY MUSCADET.

11 Bottles of claret — a Bordeaux-line case !

Make a Frenchman wine –
Kick him in the Beaujolais!

MITTERAND IS NOT THE MOST
POPULAR RED IN FRANCE.

IF WINE IS
THE FOOD OF LOVE,
I MUST BE A
SECS MANIAC.

YOU LOOK BOUZY-ROUGE :
— I'm Morgon than
I thought I was — *

As the wine grape said to the dessert grape
"I HAVE A VERY PRESSING
ENGAGEMENT!

IF ALL THE SHEILAS DRINKING COOK'S NEW ZEALAND WINE TONIGHT WERE LAID END TO END, I SHOULDN'T BE AT ALL SURPRISED.

Dry Wines have Secs appeal!

The bouquets of fine wines usually come from Interflora.

JPS

I ordered a BEAUNE because I'm on the straight and marrow.

I THOUGHT A BAG-IN-THE-BOX WAS MY DECEASED MOTHER IN LAW, UNTIL I DISCOVERED THE AUSSIE 'BLADDER PACK'

She shall have MUSAR wherever she goes

NO SECS PLEASE - WE'RE BRUTISH

I MET A BARMAID RECENTLY
WHO CHAMPAGNED BECAUSE
A STOUT PORTER BITTER!

- Methuselah is alive and well and hiding in Reims.

Yquem, Ysaw,
Yconquered.

ROLL OUT THE BARREL,
LET'S HAVE A
BAROLO FUN

UNTIL I WENT TO BURGUNDY I THOUGHT THE COTES DE NUITS WAS AN EVENING JACKET.

TORRES WINE doesn't Costa Fortune.

Claret — just what Medoc ordered.

She said she loved me but I don't think she was Sancerre.

I thought Taylors made clothes until I discovered Port.
*·!! They should stick to Clothes!

GO TO EGYPT—
DRINK DHOWS

LORRIES
OF TORRES
ARE GOOD
FOR YOUR
WORRIES!

PROCRASTINATION IS THE ART
OF SAVING YOUR BEST WINE
'TILL THE GUESTS HAVE LEFT

CIDER WITH ROSIE MAKES SOMERSET MAUGHAN!

METHODIST AIRWAYS
— DRY FLY —

DRUNKEN SPEECH IS IN THE VINACULAR

Bardolino —
What Shakespeare
had on his
bathroom floor!

I thought maceration carbonique was French for indigestion
IS PIEMONT BRUT AN ITALIAN AFTERSHAVE?
THE MORE YOU DRINK WINE, THE MORE YOU ENJOY SECS.

Amo, amas, amat, a musár!

Californian wines welcome here makes a change from lukewarm beer.

WHAT DO YOU GET IF YOU DRINK GERMAN WINES TOO FAST?
— Hock ups! —

I Quincy a pink elephant
— Reuilly?

Spanish wines rule - Olé?
French wines rule
— Bouquet?
HUNGARIAN WINES RULE
— TOKAY? —

WITH HEAVY TAX
AND VAT - IT'S NOT
JUST THE CORK
THAT GETS SCREWED!

IF YOU DON'T LIKE HOCK
OR ASTI SPUMANTE
LOOK FOR THE COCK
AND ASK FOR CHIANTI.

I LIKE GRAVES
— I prefer cremations!

THE ACCOUNTANTS WINE SOCIETY IS BUSY BOOKING THE COOK'S.

A Cork-screw is an Irish prostitute!

GRAN CORONAS IS ONLY MATCHED BY GRANPA CORONAS !

Come down to the Burgundy section, I've got a Beaune to pick with you.

IF THE WEATHER IS 'GRAVES' YOU MUST HAVE A 'MACON' OR A 'BROUILLY' WITH YOU.

NOTICE

~~TOILET CLOSED~~ PINOT !

I thought Aix en Provence was a pain in the backside.'

DID YOU KNOW THEY WERE RUNNING OUT OF BULLS IN HUNGARY?
Oenologists do it in laboratories!
IS NUITS ST. GEORGES A SECRET SOCIETY?

The Irish think "Coq au vin" is sex in a lorry.

MY GRANDMOTHER'S BEEN AGED IN WOOD
BUT SHE WAS NEVER BOTTLED.

STAY CLOSE BE CIDER WHEN YOU PLAY HEIDSIECK

TWO SWALLOWS
DON'T MAKE
A SAUMUR !

Ice in my Sherry?
Jerezy!

Hypochondriacs drink "Shampagne"

THE REAL DERIVATION OF POSH — PORT OUT, SHERRY HOME.

DO YOU LIKE RIESLING?

— I don't know. I've never Riesled.

A TORRES ADORE
IS A BULLFIGHTER
IN LOVE WITH
HIS WINE!

Harvey-Wallbanger!
Smith 4 faults!

IF YOU KEEP POURING WINE INTO A
COFFEE PERCULATOR, DO YOU GET
A PERKY COPULATOR?

MANY A BOUZY NIGHTS DRINKING
IS FOLLOWED BY AIX AND PAYNS

REDUNDANT WINE WAITERS
HAVE BEEN GIVEN
THE BARSAC!

BEAUJOLAIS —
IS THAT THE FRENCH
LEGIONAIRE WITH
THE GAMAY LEG ?

CASSONOVA
LIKED
RICCADONNA

I have an educated palate,
but paint makes the wine taste nasty!

(DOCTOR AT MORNING SURGERY)
"DO YOU HAVE A DRINK PROBLEM ?"
(PATIENT)
"It's okay thanks, I've just had a bottle."

-THE RICCA THE DONNA THE BETTER!
COOK'S NEW ZEALAND WINE IS SURE TO PLEASE, IT COMES FROM THE SUNNY ANTIPPLE-DES!
Est! Est! Est!!!
-The climactic wine
Is a Renault 4 Estate classified as a vin ordinaire?

MY PAWN BROKER KEEPS HIMSELF WELL IN HOCK.

Could an amputee grape treader from Bordeaux be said to have one foot in the Graves?

Don't take your wife into a brothel, —they'll charge you corkage!

SHE WAS ONLY A COOPERS DAUGHTER

Fractured Beaunes get you plastered!

BUT WE HAD
A BARREL
OF FUN!

FRASCATI —
Absent minded
Italian
Rennaissance
painter.

MUSAR'S WHAT IS
DRUNK BY THE
CHIC OF ARABY

WHO THOUGHT ZINFANDEL WAS A FRENCH COMEDIAN?

WOMAN — "I'VE JUST BEEN GRAPED"
POLICEMAN — "DON'T YOU MEAN RAPED?"
WOMAN — "NO,... THERE WAS A BUNCH OF THEM!

She may be
a plain dish —
but in-vino !
veri-tasty .

When grapes grow high
we Avelada.

=

WINE MERCHANTS
DO IT IN CELLARS!

Is an angry parrot, POUILLY FUMÉ?

Shampain is a pain in the Asti!

I THOUGHT BARSAC WAS A WINE UNTIL I SAW THE PUBLICANS SUIT!!

The sommelier was Soave until he Torres pants.

Does Barbara Windsor use Harveys Bristol Cream?

LEONARD ROSSITER SOAKED IN A VAT OF WHITE WINE IS A CASE OF RIESLING DAMP!

Petill-ant, a small carniverous insect!

Flash Harry drinks Champagne, —Flasher Harry prefers a Mâcon.

MAKING LOVE AND OPENING CHAMPAGNE ARE THE SAME, TOO MUCH HASTE AND YOU POP YOUR CORK, AND WASTE MOST OF IT.

TOO MUCH POUILLY, MAKES ONE FUISSÉ!

A SIP IN TIME SAVES WINE!

I never mention the Widow Clicquot when talking to Mumm

WINE DRINKERS DON'T GO ON PUB CRAWLS, — THEY GO ON Cook's Tours!

DREGS? that's what he sediment!

CLOSING TIME IS THE BITTER END.
Bucks fizziness a.m.
f...s business p.m!
IF SHE HAS A BUN
IN THE AUVERGNE
IT'LL BE HER FIRST BEARN
JPS

Diagnosis ad hock deplored by Medoc.

Drink a pinta Muscadet!

Dick Anter
is innocent,
O.K. ?

- HOPE YOU ARE TOKAY
ALL FOR NOW
YOURS SANCERRELY,

...TO KEEP IN THE 'SPIRIT' OF THINGS:

WARNINKS IS A DEVILS' ADVOCAAT

Ouzo 'fraid of the big bad wolf?

IRISH MIST IS LIKE SCOTCH, BUT THICKER'

Vat 69 is not a sex tax
— but it taxes your sex!

I told the barman my world was falling apart.
— he silently passed me a screwdriver.

MY DOCTOR TOLD ME PIMMS AND NEEDLES
ARE JUST SHAM PAIN.

GLOSSARY

ABSINTHE (Ab-santh) A very potent liqueur flavoured with anise and wormwood and generally now banned in western Europe because of the harmful affects of the wormwood. The best known of all was Pernod which enjoyed tremendous success in the 1890s and early this century and this brand, of course, flourishes today with its anis (q.v.).

ACETIC (Ass-ee-tick) An acid always present in wine to a limited extent. It can be a serious problem when found in large quantities, as it is the predominant acid of vinegar. To be avoided at all costs, mainly through careful winemaking and airtight containers.

AIX-EN-PROVENCE (Aches-on-Pro-vawnce) The ancient capital of Provence, in the south of France, which today produces a variety of lesser wines of which the rosés are undoubtedly the best.

AMOROSO (Am-oar-oh-so) A sweet style of sherry produced mainly for the British and northern European markets. Often known as a "cream" sherry and simply not served in Jerez (q.v.), where all sherry is taken dry, whether the lighter fino or darker, richer oloroso. The sweeter styles are preferred by those in colder, northern climates.

ANIS (A-neece) A popular liqueur flavoured primarily by the seeds of the anise plant and drunk in large quantities in France, Spain and most eastern Mediterranean countries. Such names as Pastis (France), Ouzo (Greece), Anis (Spain), Raki (Turkey) and Arack (Lebanon) will be seen. It turns cloudy white when water is added. Similar to the more potent Absinthe (q.v.).

ANJOU (Awn-joo) A very large area in the centre of the Loire River Valley of northwestern France. The good whites range from the unusual dry Savennières on the north bank of the Loire to the intensely sweet and long-lived wines of the Coteaux du Layon to the south. Lots of good rosé and, in Saumur, some of the best sparkling wine outside Champagne, made by the same method, are produced.

APPELLATION CONTROLEE (Appel-ass-yon Control-lay) Literally "Controlled name". Although generally thought to be a guarantee of quality, it is in reality a fairly complicated series of laws which assure one that the wine comes from the region stated and is made by "traditional methods". Whether that wine is of high quality cannot, alas, be controlled by legislation.

ARMAGNAC (Ar-man-yack) France's second best-known Brandy, made in southwestern France. Usually quite full-bodied, pungent and dry.

ASTI A small town in the northwestern Piedmont region of Italy and the centre of Italian sparkling (Spumante) wine production. The wines range from fairly dry to quite sweet and are made mainly from the grapey Moscato (q.v.) grape.

BARBERA (Bar-bair-a) A black grape, Italian in origin, and used especially in the Piedmont region of northwest Italy. Also now seen in New World countries, where it can make excellent, robust wine.

BARDOLINO (Bar-doe-leeno) A light fresh and fruity wine made on the eastern shores of Lake Garda in Italy's Veneto region. Similar in style, though lighter in colour and weight to the wines of Valpolicella.

BAROLO (Ba-row-low) Robust, full-bodied red wine, from the Piedmont region. Often thought to be the finest Italian wine of all, it requires considerable ageing to be at its best. Tasters regularly detect a "tariness" when assessing Barolo, and it is definitely an acquired taste.

BARSAC (Bar-sack) Good sweet dessert wine made in Bordeaux. Like all fine sweet table wines, Barsac owes its quality to the curiously named "Noble Rot" (q.v.).

BAUME (Bow-may) A scale of sweetness widely used to express the density of the must (unfermented grape juice). The sweeter the must, the more alcoholic the wine will be.

BEARN (Bairn) The old French name for the province which borders the Pyrennees in the west. Its best-known wines are those of Jurançon.

BEAUJOLAIS (Bow-jo-lay) One of the most popular red wines of France. Light, fresh and very fruity, if often represents good value and is generally available in considerable quantity—so much in some years that a saying has evolved that "Three rivers flow into Lyon—the Rhône, the Saône and the Beaujolais".

BEAUNE (Bone) The "Capital" city of Burgundy and one of its finest vineyard areas.

BLANC (Blonk) French for white, and used in many ways on labels of French wines. Most common is "Blanc de Blancs" which simply means white wine made from white grapes. Sounds only logical, perhaps, but it is perfectly possible to make a white wine from black grapes provided the juice is not allowed any contact with the grape skins which contain all the pigment.

BOMMES (Bom) A small village which gives its name to a commune within the Sauternes (q.v.) district of Bordeaux.

BONNEZEAUX (Bawn-e-zoh) One of the finest of the sweet Coteaux du Layon vineyards (see Anjou) and entitled to its own Appellation Contrôlée (q.v.).

BOUZY (Boozey) The humorous name of a small village in the centre of the Champagne region where red grapes, used for the production of Champagne and a still red wine (Bouzy Rouge) are grown.

BROUILLY (Brew-yee) The southernmost of the Beaujolais cru villages (q.v.), making a lighter style than most.

BRUT (Brute) Whereas 'sec' (q.v.) means dry throughout most of France, you must look for 'brut' on a bottle of Champagne if you want it to be really dry. Considered, especially by the British, to be the finest.

BUTT The standard cask used in Jerez (q.v.) for the storage and maturation of sherry. A shipping butt holds 108 imperial gallons while the larger bodega (warehouse) butt holds approximately 140 gallons.

CABERNET (Cab-air-nay) One of the great red wine grapes. Usually refers to the Cabernet Sauvignon, although Cabernet Franc is also important. Highly successful throughout the wine-producing world, but arguably at its best in Bordeaux.

CHABLIS (Shab-lee) One of the best known of all white burgundies and located not in the main Côte d'Or (q.v.) district, but 100 km northwest on the banks of the River Yonne. Crisp, fresh and flinty-dry, the wines can achieve great finesse, particularly the Grand Cru (q.v.).

CHAI (Shay) A building in which wine is stored at ground level. Not to be confused with a cave (kahv) where wines are kept in underground cellars.

CHAMBERTIN (Shom-bare-tan) One of the greatest (many would say **the** greatest) red burgundies. Preferred by Napoleon during his frequent military strolls through the region.

CHASSELAS (Shas-e-lah) A table grape which is popular throughout Europe and which is also used to make light, usually indifferent wines.

CHATEAU (Shat-oh) A word widely used throughout France, but particularly in Bordeaux, to denote the wine of a single property, made at the property, from grapes grown at the property. Although all the finest clarets (q.v.) come from single châteaux the corollary that château produced wine is automatically of higher quality does not always hold true. Often a well-made blended Bordeaux Rouge from a reputable shipper will be superior to many ordinary wines that carry a château name.

A list of some of the Bordeaux château mentioned in this book follows:

CH. CHEVAL BLANC (Shevall Blonk)—One of the best wines of the St. Emilion district which is adjacent to Pomerol (q.v.).

CH. FILHOT (Fee-oh)—An excellent Sauternes (q.v.) which is distinctive in being somewhat drier than most (a relative statement only).

CH. GLORIA—A consistently good, though not classified growth (i.e. the 1855 classification) from the St. Julian commune of the Médoc (q.v.).

CH. HAUT BRION (Oh Bree-ohn)—The best red wine of Graves (q.v.) and uniquely included in the 1855 classification of the great wines of the Médoc.

CH. LAFITE (La-feet)—Arguably one of Bordeaux's greatest wines, Lafite is always listed first of the first growths and, particularly in the best years, is reckoned by many to make the finest claret of all.

CH. LATOUR—One of the four original first growths of the Médoc. Like Château Lafite, it is located in the commune of Pauillac (Poy-ack), and it tends to be a big, fairly tough wine which requires many years to reach its peak.

CH. LOUDENNE (Loo-den)—A well-publicised property in the Médoc owned by a large multi-national wine and spirit corporation.

CH. MARGAUX (Mar-go)—A wine which is more delicate and 'feminine' than the other first growths.

CH. MOUTON-ROTHSCHILD (Mootonn Roth-cheeld)—This fine château was not included in the original 1855 classification, and a motto evolved which, translated, stated "First I cannot be, Second I do not deign to be, I am Mouton". However, as a reward for the years of campaigning by the property's current owner, the French government decreed in 1973 that Mouton is now a first growth.

CH. PALMER—An excellent property in the commune of Margaux which regularly achieves prices that are among the highest in Bordeaux, save those of the first growths.

CH. PAPE CLEMENT (Pahp Clay-mont)—An excellent red wine from the Graves (q.v.) district.

CH. YQUEM (Ee-kem)—The finest sweet wine of Bordeaux, Yquem reaches heights other wines only dream of. The prices it fetches are also the stuff of dreams (nightmares!).

The use of the word Château is not confined to Bordeaux, and appears fairly regularly throughout France, viz:

CH. GRILLET (Gree-yay)—A very rare and expensive white wine from the northern Rhône valley that has the distinction of being the smallest vineyard area with its own Appellation Contrôlée (q.v.). The vineyard covers less than four acres.

CHATEAUNEUF-DU-PAPE (Shat-oh-nerf-Doo-Pap)—A district in the southern Rhône Valley where robust red (and some white) wines are produced. The rules which have governed its production since 1923 were followed by the national authorities in 1936, when they created the laws of Appellation Contrôlée.

CHENAS (Shane-ah)   One of the nine "crus" (q.v.) of Beaujolais (q.v.).

CHIANTI (Key-anti)   The most famous red wine of Tuscany in central Italy. It can be of excellent quality if from the 'classico' region, which is denoted by a seal on every bottle featuring a black cockerel.

CHIROUBLES (Shear-roobl)   Another part of the Beaujolais "cru" (q.v.).

CLARET   The Englishman's term for red Bordeaux wine.

CONDOM   A small village in the centre of the Armagnac (q.v.) region of south-west France, which produces the finest Armagnac brandies. (For other definitions, ask your chemist!)

COOKS   See the Foreword by John Arlott.

CORTON   The small vineyard area which produces the finest red wines of the Côte de Beaune (q.v.) in Burgundy. The white wines of the district, known as Corton-Charlemagne, are also amongst the best of Burgundy.

COTE (Coat)   A French term for a slope with vineyards.

COTE D'OR (Coat Door)   "The Golden Slope" from which comes all of Burgundy's finest red wines and most of her best whites. Further divided into the Côtes de Nuits (Coat de Nwee) in the north and the Côtes de Beaune (Coat de Bone) in the south.

CRU (Croo)   "Growth" in French—it refers to a specific vineyard. A Cru Classé, therefore, is a classified growth and a Grand Cru, a great one. When applied to the wines of Beaujolais, cru refers to the wines of nine specific villages in the northern part of the region where the finest wines are made.

DOLE   A red wine produced from the Gamay (q.v.) grape in the Valais region of southern Switzerland.

DOSAGE (Doh-sahj)   The French term which refers to the addition of a small amount of sweetening wine to a dry sparkling wine prior to its final corking and labelling.

DOURO (Doo-row)   The river in northern Portugal which is the home of Port. The wine got its name from the city at the mouth of the Douro, Oporto.

DOUX (Doo)   French for sweet. The other end of the scale from sec (q.v.), except in Champagne, where brut (q.v.) is the driest.

EST! EST!! EST!!!   A white wine (both dry and medium-dry) produced in central Italy about 50 miles north of Rome. Its name originates from the travels of a 12th century German bishop who liked his wine so much that he sent a servant ahead to sample the wines available at inns on his route. The taster then marked either Est (It is) for good wine or Non Est (It is not), for all others on the wall of the establishment. One so impressed him, that he gave it a "three star rating" that survives today on the labels of this wine.

FIXIN (Fee-san)   A tiny village in the northernmost end of the Côte de Nuits (q.v.). Rarely seen under its own name, it usually ends up in blends which carry the Appellation Côte de Nuits.

FLOR   Spanish for 'flower' and used to describe the variety of yeast which forms naturally on the surface of some sherry while maturing in cask and which gives that wine the flowery, dry 'fino' character.

FRASCATI (Fras-car-tee)   A dry white wine made just south of Rome.

GAMAY   The red grape responsible for the delightful wines of Beaujolais (q.v.). Although in other parts of Burgundy (and indeed, the world) it produces very indifferent bottles, in the Beaujolais it reaches admirable heights, particularly in the "cru" (q.v.) villages.

GAY LUSSAC (Loo-sack)   A French chemist whose formula for alcoholic fermentation is accepted as the classic. He also developed an alcoholometer and the strength of wines and spirits is often referred to as "degrees Gay Lussac". In metric terms, for this read "percentage of alcohol by volume".

GIGONDAS (Jee-gond-ahs)   Robust red wine made in the southern Rhône, from the same selection of grape varieties as used in Châteauneuf-du-Pape (q.v.).

GRAVES (Grahv)   A district in Bordeaux in which both good dry red and dry white and average sweetish white wines are produced. Its soil is a mixture of gravel and sand hence the name. Its best known property, Château Haut-Brion (q.v.), although not in the Médoc (q.v.) was so highly regarded as to be included in the famous 1855 classification of the best vineyards of the Médoc.

GRENACHE (Greh-nash)   A black wine grape used widely throughout southern France and in Spain. It gives wines a high alcohol content and fairly assertive character.

HOCK   The Englishman's name for German Rhine wines. Originally referring to the wines of Hochheim, near Wiesbaden, which was a favourite watering-hole of Queen Victoria, it now denotes most German wines not from the Mosel (q.v.). Hocks are usually found in brown bottles, while Moselles appear in green.

JEREZ (Hair-eth)   The centre of Sherry production in Andalucia—Spain's southern most province. Only the fortified wines of this region can be called "Sherry". Similar wines from other countries must, by law, be clearly prefixed with the country of origin—i.e. "South African Sherry".

LIEBFRAUMILCH (Leeb-frow-milsh)   The best known of all German wines. Originally from the vineyards of Liebfrauenkirche and Worms, it can now come from a number of regions and covers a multitude of sins. Generally, however, it represents standard, straightforward "hock" (q.v.).

MACERATION CARBONIQUE (Mass-er-assee-on Car-bon-eek)   A method of making wine, practised widely in Beaujolais, the Rhône and southern France. By keeping the grapes in an atmosphere of carbon dioxide during fermentation, an extremely fruity and fast-developing wine results. A well-known example is Beaujolais Nouveau.

MACON (Mack-on)   Burgundy's predominantly white wine area south of the small Côte d'Or (q.v.). One of its most famous villages is Fuissé (of Pouilly Fuissé fame).

MARC (Mar)   A spirit distilled from the residue of grape pressings. The spent grape skins are mixed with water and the resultant liquid is then converted to a fairly potent, yet distinctive liquor that, with cask ageing, can achieve quite good quality.

MARSALA (Mahr-sahla)   A sweet, fortified dessert wine made in Sicily which comes in several styles and qualities. Nelson's Royal Navy used to drink Marsala regularly.

MEDOC (Meh-doc)   The best-known district within the Bordeaux region, and one that produces only red wine. The area, which is located on the left bank of the Gironde River, was the subject of an exhaustive classification in 1855 which essentially holds true even today.

MERLOT (Mair-low)   A black grape used in Bordeaux to soften the wines made mainly from the Cabernet Sauvignon (q.v.). In Pomerol (q.v.) and St. Emilion, however, it is the predominant variety. Also grown successfully in other parts of the world, particularly Italy.

MEURSAULT (Myrh-so)   One of Burgundy's finest white wines, made from the Chardonnay grape in the southern Côte de Beaune (q.v.). With ageing, the wines develop a very full, distinctive bouquet and flavour.

METHUSELAH (Meth-oo-salah)   Why the champagne shippers name their very large bottles after Biblical figures is unclear, but this giant holds the equivalent of eight standard bottles. Larger than a Jeroboam (four bottles) but a mere David against the Goliath of Reims and Epernay—the Nebuchadnessar—which holds twenty bottles and which takes a real Goliath just to lift it, let alone pour it!

MINERVOIS (Meen-air-vwa)   A large wine producing area of south west France, to the northwest of Narbonne. Red wine is made here which in its best form benefits from some ageing.

MIS EN BOUTEILLE (Meez-on-Boo-tai)   Literally "Bottled" in French and a term seen often on labels, suffixed by such phrases as 'au Château' (at the Château); 'à Domaine' (at the Domaine); 'dans nos caves' (in our cellars).

MOSELLE (Mo-zell)   The wine produced on the Mosel River in Germany. Generally they are lighter and more delicate than the "hocks" (q.v.) of the Rhein. The better wines are all made from the classic Riesling (q.v.) grape on the incredibly steep slopes of the Mosel valley.

MULLER-THURGAU (Miller-Tur-gow)   A white wine grape which is a cross between sub-varieties of the Riesling (q.v.) and named after the Swiss Doctor Müller of the Canton of Thurgau who first established the cross. Quite grapey and flowery, it is now the most widely used variety in Germany and also makes good wines throughout the world.

MUSAR   See Foreword by John Arlott.

MUSCADET (Moosk-a-day)   The bone-dry white wine of Britany made in the vineyards around Nantes, where the Loire river flows into the Atlantic. Hardly known outside the region several decades ago, it is now recognised as the ideal accompaniment to fish and seafood. The best Muscadets are sold "Sur Lie" (q.v.) and come from the Sevre-et-Maine area.

MUSCAT (Moos-kah)   A family of wine grapes, usually red or black, which flourishes everywhere wine is made. One of the few varieties that produces a wine which actually smells and tastes like grapes. Dry to sweet; still, fortified and sparkling. Also known as Moscato, Moscatel, etc.

NOBLE ROT   "Pourriture Noble" (q.v.) in French. The beneficial mildew, Botrytis Cinerea, that can affect ripe grapes at harvest-time and reduce their water content, thereby greatly increasing the sugar and giving the winemaker a must (unfermented grape juice) which will produce superb dessert wine. Best known examples: Sauternes, Barsac, Beeren- and Trockenbeerenauslesen wines from Germany and Austria.

OENOLOGIST   (Een-ologist)   A wine-maker, or wine technologist.

PEDRO XIMENEZ (Pay-dro Hee-men-eth)   A sweet white wine grape grown mainly in Spain and which is used in Jerez (q.v.) in the making of Sherry.

PETTILLANT (Petty-ohn)   The French term for a wine which is very slightly sparkling, due to a final fermentation in bottle resulting in a small amount of CO_2 being retained in the wine. Usually only perceptible as a slight "prickle" on the tongue.

PHYLLOXERA (Fill-ox-era)   A louse of the vine, originating in America, which, in the late 19th century, totally devastated the vineyards of Europe, then the world. The only effective long-term way of combating the pest is to graft a European vine onto an American root-stock.

PIESPORT (Pees-port)   A diminutive village on the Mosel (q.v.) river in Germany which can produce wines of considerable quality but often today is seen on fairly indifferent Moselles made from the flat, sweeping vineyards on the opposite side of the river.

PINOT (Pee-no)   A very distinguished family of wine grapes used throughout the world, but especially in Burgundy and Champagne. The black variety, the Pinot Noir, is responsible for all the great red wines of the Côte d'Or (q.v.) and is also widely used in Champagne. Rarely successful in other parts of the world, however, the Pinot Blanc, with the Noir, is widely used in Champagne, while the Pinot Gris (Gree), known in Alsace as the Tokay d'Alsace and in Germany as the Ruhländer (Roo-lender) makes quite rich, full-bodied wines.

POMEROL   A small district in Bordeaux which borders the better known St. Emilion. It produces some of the richest, most appealing clarets, the best of which, Château Pétrus, often achieves the highest prices of all in the auction rooms.

POUILLY FUME (Pwee Foo-may)   Distinctive dry white wine from the eastern Loire Valley. Virtually adjacent, and very similar in style, to Sancerre (q.v.). Not to be confused with the white burgundies of Pouilly Fuissé (q.v.).

POURRITURE NOBLE (Poor-ee-tour Nob-l)   See 'Noble Rot'.

QUINCY (Can-see)   A small district of the Loire, somewhat removed from the rest of the vineyard areas, and whose wines are similar in style to those of Sancerre (q.v.) and Pouilly (q.v.).

REIMS (Ranss)   One of the two centres of the Champagne trade, the other being Epernay (Ep-air-nay). The City has one of the most beautiful cathedrals in Europe which saw the coronation of French Kings for a thousand years.

RETSINA (Ret-see-nah)   A Greek wine which has a resinous taste because it has been treated with pine resin. Particularly good with the oily food of the country.

REUILLY (Rhu-yee)   A small vineyard area near Quincy (q.v.) in the Loire region whose wines resemble its near neighbour.

RIESLING (Reez-ling)   One of the world's classic white grape varieties, at its best in Alsace, Mosel and Rhein vineyards. Its wines are always fruity and delicate and can make superb sweet wines if affected by 'noble rot' (q.v.). Outside Germany and France the vine is usually referred to as Rheinriesling to distinguish it from its most common derivative, the Italian or Welschriesling.

RIOJA (Ree-och-ah) Spain's premier table wine district, located n the Basque country along the Ebro River. The quality of the wines owes something to the fact that the growers and winemakers of today are the descendants of those who fled the phylloxera (q.v.) infestation of Bordeaux in the 1870s.

SAKI (Sah-key) Japanese rice-wine usually served warm in small cups. Distinctly potent.

SANCERRE (Son-sair) With its twin town of Pouilly on the Loire river, this area produces one of the most distinctive white wines of France. The Sauvignon Blanc grape here seems to display its most forceful and appealing characteristics. Intensely fruity with an almost "smoky" overtone.

SPANNA A good red wine from northwest Italy made from the Nebbiolo grape—the same variety that is responsible for Barolo (q.v.).

SAVIGNY-LES-BEAUNE (Sah-veen-yee-lay-Bone) A commune within the famous Beaune (q.v.) district which produces quite light, but elegant red wines and a small amount of good white burgundy.

SCHLOSS (Shlos) German for 'castle' and the equivalent in the Rhein or Mosel to a "Château" in France.

SEC French for dry. Whilst this holds true for table wines, a sec sparkling wine will be sweeter than its brut (q.v.) counterpart. Can also be modified (i.e. Demi-sec = "Medium-dry").

SEKT German sparkling wine (if called Deutscher Sekt) and more often today merely sparkling wine made in Germany from grapes that were grown elsewhere (usually Italy). Ranges from quite pleasant to distinctly un.

SOAVE (Swarvay) Italy's most famous white wine, produced in the Veneto region. Agreeably dry yet soft, the wine never reaches great heights but provides refreshing drinking in considerable quantity.

SUR LIE (Soor Lee) Literally 'on its lees', the phrase refers to any wine left in cask to mature on the spent yeast cells, or 'lees', which are the end product of fermentation. Most common in Muscadet (q.v.) where it results in a fuller, somewhat richer wine.

SYLVANER (Sill-varner) A prolific German grape variety that used to account for much of the lesser wines of that country. Today, being largely replaced by Müller Thurgau (q.v.).

SYRAH (See-rah) A fine black wine grape at its best in the northern Rhône, but successfully grown around the world, particularly in Australia, where it is called the Shiraz.

TOKAY (Toe-kai) Hungary's most celebrated wine. In its best form, it is an intensely sweet and highly flavoured wine that reminds some tasters of apricots. The precious Tokay Essence, of which very little is ever made, used to be jealously guarded in the cellars of Kings and Princes of Europe.

TORRES See Foreword by John Arlott.

TRAMINER (Tra-meener) More commonly referred to as the Gewürztraminer, or 'spicy' Traminer. This is a white wine grape that makes an intensely fruity and aromatic wine. Probably at its best in Alsace.

V.D.Q.S.—VIN DELIMITES DE QUALITE SUPERIEURE A French quality designation one step below Appellation Contrôlée (q.v.). These 'second division' wines are subject to many of the same controls as imposed by the A.C. laws and the best are sometimes promoted into the 'first division' just as some Vins de Pays (q.v.) are eventually elevated to V.D.Q.S. status.

VENTOUX (Von-too) Côtes de Ventoux—A region in the southern Rhône that, like nearby Gigondas (q.v.), produces good, full-bodied red wine.

VINS DE PAYS (Van de Pay) Literally, wines of the country, these wines are produced mainly in the south of France and are often sound wines of some regional character. Subject, in theory, to a considerable range of controls, the wines can appear to be merely well-packaged and somewhat dearer Vin Ordinaire.

VOUVRAY (Voo-vray) The classic white Loire wine of Touraine. Made from the Chenin Blanc grape, it can come in many styles, but the finest are the sweet wines which mature admirably. Good sparkling wines are also produced here.

ZINFANDEL Although thought to be Italian in origin, this popular red grape produces lots of good, robust wine in California, which may occasionally seem strange to European palates.

CUT HERE.

YOUR NAME
& ADDRESS

_____

_____

_____

Send your contributions to :
THE WINE GRAFFITI BOOK.
186 SLOANE STREET · LONDON SW1 · ENGLAND